BUDGET FASHION WARDROBE

RASHI SAINI

BUDGET

FASHION

WARDROBE

RASHI SAINI

BUDGET FASHION WARDROBE

*Content*_______________________

Chapter 1   Budget Fashion Wardrobe

Chapter 2   I define "Budget Fashion Wardrobe"

Chapter 3   **Why** you should have Budget fashion wardrobe

Chapter 4   **HOW** to get Budget Fashion wardrobe

Chapter 5   **WHAT** to EXACTLY get into the wardrobe Finally!!!

Budget Fashion Wardrobe

We all girls have that one dream of having a wardrobe like Kardashian sisters. A wardrobe with lots of clothes and especially having the shoe corner where there would be forty to sixty pair of heels and beautiful footwear. A wardrobe as shown in the series 'sex in the city' is defiantly on so many girl's lists as a part of their house. Having all the trending clothes and bags of those classic brands like Gucci, Chanel, Zara and so many in your wardrobe is so many girl's dreams.

I agree having these big wardrobe sounds cool but having it practically is little difficult. Because most of the time we have a limit barrier to our pockets and having these really huge wardrobes costs a lot. But we all love fashion, ladies!! A love which we can never leave because it is just so irresistible.

In that situation having a fashionable wardrobe under budget will always be there to make us look real fashionable ladies. Budget fashion wardrobe will not for sure be having stacks of heels but will definitely be having everything that will never let you go out of fashion.

define "Budget Fashion Wardrobe " as __________

> " Budget fashion wardrobe is something which includes specific items, items which allow you doing RATIONAL STYLING"

Being specific to the items which will be there in your wardrobe is really important. The idea of the specific item is that that to be accurate of your requirements and not to be overly expensive. It's really important for the specific items not to be overly expensive because you have to be in your budget and fulfill all requirements which include basic necessity, fashion trends, designs that you love. These all should be included in your closet under a decent budget price range.

To accomplish the above task it is very important to understand the concept of rational styling because this will pave the pathway for the entry of your fashion to get into your closet. Rational styling means you being very aware of your needs and very specific about yourself. These both things are very important in the twentieth century because the advertisements around us these days are being really manipulative and are just busy selling their products and techniques at the cost of your self confidence.

Fashion is something that is meant to uplift your confidence and to present your personality in a more enhanced way. But today's fashion world is doing something that is a little opposite to the basic concept of fashion.

The fashion market is huge, really huge place so there is a need to have a proper navigation system for yourself which gonna prevent you from getting lost in this place and being taken in by someone.

Rational styling is that tool which will help you throughout this huge place of fashion. Being aware of your requirements will never let you invest your money into something that would not be of worth and being specific about yourself will protect you from being manipulated. Manipulation like about the right body type, right color, right dress, the right way of wearing, the right hair, right eyes, right skin and the list is endless are present at every step in this place and many women are unknowingly caught into this manipulation cycle. I don't want my readers to be the victim of such bad game after learning the skills I will be telling you in this book.

Why you should have Budget fashion wardrobe

Being a 20th-century lady, here are the reasons why you should have a budget fashion wardrobe.

There are top 10 reasons I have mentioned below WHY it is so important for you to have budget fashion wardrobe and I want you to read each point very carefully because these points are like telling you how that one secret ingredient makes a dish so delicious. So get ready to know how that secret ingredient sounds like and be the real fashionable lady

- It makes you a smart lady

- Don't be ashamed of having such wardrobe because it shows that you believe in making a smart investment.

- It makes you look intelligent in your group as you will be having the best clothes without spending too much money.

- It saves your time. You won't be wasting your time being confused in figuring out what to wear from the heap of meaningless clothes.

- It prevents you from buying garbage from the market, means that it will prevent you from buying things which you think you might wear someday but end up not wearing them at all.

- If you are a busy lady but loves fashion and don't have time for shopping so keeping up this type of wardrobe will really help you in saving time while shopping. As you will read this book further you will figure out how this saves your lot of time.

- You will know your style better than any other. This means you won't need those so-called stylist suggestions and advice to know what looks best on you.

- When you don't buy those overly priced clothes while shopping with your boyfriend because you believe in RATIONAL STYLING being a fashionable lady and you tell this to him as the reason , this will make him having a more hard crush on you because you sound smart and a more pragmatic person ....and a someone who can handle his expenses quite well. Trust me this happens, good observant catches everything.

- Makes you most trendy person.Having a limited and accurate items makes you smart to choose the right thing at the right time.

- Help you having trash out of your closet , as most of the time the closet's one-third space is always occupied by the clothes that you don't wear.

At last, you will end up having a really good collection of clothes, footwear, bags and jewelleries both in quantity and quality. What else do we want being a fashion lover!!!

HOW to get Budget Fashion wardrobe

I will be telling you the exact 4 techniques which will be guiding you in "HOW"to create a budget fashion wardrobe.

1. "DO NOT" Considering your body shape

Ya exactly, do not consider your body shape. From body shape, I mean all those terms like pear shape body, apple shape body, triangular or inverted triangular body type and so many on the list.

When for the first time I came across these terms I got so fascinated and thought that I got the solution to all my problems of choosing the right design pattern which will suit my body. I worked really hard to understand these shapes and tried lot of things accordingly to those body shape manuals but I realized that it didn't work that accurate the way it sounded in those books and videos and so I being a science student I dived into finding the science behind it on which this theory was developed. I was amazed by the results of my research, the results were shocking because it did not have any strong scientific logic behind these body type concepts. So after my research on the internet, I thought to take my own observations again. So I tried many clothes but this time made two sections, the first section was for the clothes I randomly liked and the second column was for the clothes mentioned in the manuals of the body type. I tried the clothes and tried to observe any visual difference I could come up for my body shape , even made my friends to observe and find any difference they could get, but the results were not up to the mark. It didn't make the difference till the extends the manuals mentioned and still telling ladies that how greatly they are important to us.

After all my research work I finally end up to the conclusion that it does not matter whichever your body type you have, wear clothes that you like because the clothes which you will like will definitely enhance your body shape.

It is correctly said that "fashion is not what you wear but it is the confidence you wear when you dress up". It is the confidence that helps to show your personality in a more better way.

The theory of having clothes according to your body shape has been disproof by so many plus-size models these days in fashion industries. One of the most prominent and my favourite model Ashley Graham has disproof this theory in amazing ways, she is a plus size lady and still having the sizes way too beyond the standard sizes of models asked in fashion industry, she is successful in creating a benchmark for models by being on the cover of various big fashion magazines and featured as fitness model. She even did a video with glamour magazine on youtube titling " How to wear everything you have been told not to". It was amazing to see her wearing all those things which these body shape manuals say not to wear by the ladies of her shape, you should watch it .For example, I will pick one of the famous ones,so it is said by these body shape guidelines that ladies with broad shoulders should not prefer wearing horizontal patterned dresses or tops, but Ashley Graham did wear the horizontal patterned top and prove it completely wrong advice and showed how confidence and your attitude towards yourself is the most important thing.

As I said Budget fashion includes "Rational styling" so we need to think rationally. Don't be ashamed of your body just because it is not exactly like traditional models. As I said before, fashion is a really a huge place so you need to find the clothes which you will love and it very important to know the fashion you like because your fashion taste is so individual and unique as it represents you.
With this we arrive to our second technique for how to get budget fashion wardrobe.

2. Mirror Technique

This technique is very important. Being a fashionista we all want to be the influencer of fashion in some way, big or small, but want to be that influencer somewhere inside us ,to who's style people around us would love to try. So this second technique helps you to be the influencer too.

That is why this technique is important because it gives a bonus also i.e being an influencer. In this technique, you learn about the BEST features about yourself.To make yourself aware of your best beauty features.

Now! You might be wondering how is this even relatable to having a wardrobe.

When you make your portfolio or a job resume, what do you put in it? Do you put your best work and mention things you find yourself good at?
Of course YES!!
No one would mention things in their resumes in which they are not that good enough.

Similarly, fashion is exactly like preparing your job resume. So if you don't know the positive aspects of your look, how would you be able to put it and present it in front of others.

So to have a good fashionable presentation you need to highlight the strong aspects of your personality.
This is how you get to know about your positive aspect by sitting in front of the mirror. That is why it is named so! Make yourself sit in front of the mirror. Then you have to observe yourself, keenly observe your every detail you could see in the mirror.
But a BIG WARNING!! before that, you have to keep all your negative thoughts, ideas aside. Even if how strongly you feel some negative thoughts about yourself, make it go quite for a while, you have to do it at any cost before proceeding in this technique. Make your negative subconscious silent for some time.

And now, you can start with your face. Observe the shape of it, is round like Selena Gomez or long like Angelina Jolie or cute fluffy face like Demi Levato.It can be of any shape, what is important is that you have an idea about the shape of your face.

Observe every detail and admire it because those details are your uniqueness and make the strongest point about your fashion as you know a good fashion is that which is unique too. So look if your forehead is kinda broad or high like Rihanna or it is like Jennifer Lopez. Having straight eyebrows giving you smart and bold look or having really angular eyebrows giving you sexy look or having light eyebrows giving you soft and decent look. Observe your lips, and praise them for how perfect they are for your perfect kiss. Longneck or short neck on which you can have beautiful necklaces. Look at your hands, those hard-working hands, which help you get the good fabric for your clothes. Look at them and think, how artistic and dramatic will your hands look if it gets some big rings on your fingers or could be small rings which will make your hands look more decent. There are numerous little details which are so beautiful, they just need your attention, explore them, explore your beauty. When you will get to know about them then you will finally be able to get yourself into a fashion which will enhance your beauty points.
And ya, never forget to observe the positioning of your moles, they all are sexy, so don't miss them.

Finally, by learning this technique you will be even more specific about your styling.

But this technique needs one skill. The skill is self-admiration and stopping self-criticism. And as like all other skill in the world, you learn it by practicing. So you need to practice it by finding at least one thing in your look, which you will admire by looking in the mirror and complimenting yourself during the day. By practicing this you will become skillful and you will able to utilize the technique in its best way. Because this makes you more accurate about your styling.

3. Coloring Your Mood

It is one of the most fun technique of all. It asks you to give color to your mood. It means that what kind of vibes you get when you think about a certain color. Like, when I think of the black color to wear, moods like being sexy,bold or clever hits my brain. Similarly, there are different vibes that you get when you think about a certain color to wear.

It was so fun for me when I was working on this technique. It gave me an opportunity to explore my ways of perceiving things around me. I never realized before this, the way I used to take things. For me, understanding fashion from this perspective always gave me the opportunity to understand myself in a better way. When I was on this path of understanding fashion from this perspective, I was very sure that I am on the right route. I can proof you that this way of taking fashion is the right way ,by explaining you one basic observation we have but hardly notice. It is as follows.

What we think about an art? Art is something at which the artist tries to paint his thoughts, idea or perspective. Art is a work of thought which comes out in the form of various color and forms. Have you ever heard any rule book for art. There are no guiding manuals telling you how to portray a certain idea in a certain pattern. This is because an art doesn't have any limits, it depends upon the artistic creativity and the depth of the artist's thoughts. In the similar manner, the very basic fashion is also defined as the art form of dressing. So even fashion is infinite, we can not limit it, and its limitless property is proven by great creative designers every day at great fashion shows through their creativity.

The way art is meant for celebration and awareness about a certain message, fashion is also meant for celebration and awareness similarly. Every kind of art form is always very influential to the society, the great old artwork had a huge influence on the society, music is another art form which has so strong influence on the society. Theaters and movies are another big proof how art forms are so influential. In the similar manner Fashion is another art form as one of the most influential art forms.

Because these art forms are so influential, they can be considered as a really strong tool in the hands of the people, the society.
Any tool in this world became strong when you know complete knowledge about the tool, then only you can utilize the tool to its full potential.

In the fashion, you yourself are the strongest tool, so to use it to its full potential, you should know about yourself.
And hence as I said, I proof how the real fashion gives you the opportunity to explore yourself.

I strongly believe that fashion is one such platform, which allows you to learn about yourself in the most creative way. The fashion which makes you question about your natural beauty,your skin colour , your hair, your body shape and makes you feel you are not beautiful enough then I must tell you ladies that that is not fashion but the dirty marketing of fashion sector in the name of fashion, Who's aim is to just earn profit at the cost of your self-confidence and the belief of humans in true, realistic and natural beauty.

I am listing down some moods that are most commonly perceived by most of the brain when seeing that particular colour.

We will see the most basic colors, which are Black, Gray, Purple, Pink, Red, Blue, Green.

Under every color, I have mentioned some adjectives. these adjectives are the most common feelings that are generated when we see a certain color. We humans have one sensing quality where we understand through vibes, there is no need of words for experiencing it. Every color has its own vibes which we being humans perceive in a certain manner. Every color gives a different feeling, some colors give us the feeling of just being too sad and some colors look so jolly and cheerful.

So here instead of giving you the guidelines for which color you should prefer I believe in making you understand the colors, the language they speak. When we start understanding the language of colors we can use that technology to enhance the look. I believe that the person should wear colors that the person is in need of because it gives certain vibes to us and we feel those colors and start feeling in some particular way.

I like to use this technique to boost myself. Whenever I feel low, I purposely choose the bright colours to wear for that day, something bright in colour in my whole look, so whenever I look I unconsciously feel better and more confident because of the presence of the colour. This is very scientific and this all theory is based on the chemical secretion that happens in our brain when we see a certain colour.

This technique is used by all celebrity stylist to present a celebrity with the certain image in front of the audience. Its the part of the celebrity's business to come out with such type of image of a personality which could depict their idea, the values they want to spread through their work, so as to present the audience in the best way and people can understand the most authentic form behind their artwork.

In bonus with the adjectives, I have put some famous brand logos under those colors. These brand logos will help you to understand the colors vibes in a much better way. You will see that how these colors help these brands to tell the values and ideology of their company to the customers in the similar manner the celebrity do through their looks.

Let us start with BLACK

BLACK

- Sophistication
- Power
- Formality
- Sexy
- Evil
- Grief
- Classy
- Dramatic
- Bold
- stylish

GREY

- stability
- strength of character
- authority
- maturity
- glamorous
- cool

JAGUAR

Mercedes-Benz

TOYOTA

NISSAN

Audi

HYUNDAI

PURPLE

- royalty
- dignity
- wisdom
- passion
- magic
- reflective
- imaginative
- quiet

YAHOO!®

PINK

- luxury
- power
- royalty
- romance
- beauty
- love
- sensitivity
- warmth

BR
baskin
robbins®

PINK
FLOYD

VICTORIA'S SECRET

YELLOW

- energy
- cheerful
- friendliness
- Intellect
- warm
- stimulating
- active
- Hope
- optimism

BURGER
KING

i'm lovin' it

WARNER HOME VIDEO
WB

Post-it
Brand

Snapchat

SUBWAY

RED

- Energy
- Strength
- Romance
- Urgency
- Daring
- Vitality
- Courage
- excitement

Coca-Cola

Virgin

You Tube
Broadcast Yourself™

Pinterest

Levi's

BLUE

- peace
- tranquility
- calm
- integrity
- sincerity
- affection
- relaxed
- at ease
- confident

NIVEA

PayPal

Nestle

GREEN

- balance
- generous
- clarity
- positive
- relaxation
- freshness

ANDROID

Spotify

Carlsberg

ANIMAL
PLANET

Now you get a better understanding of how colors work on our brain. So next time when you are going for shopping, instead of thinking which color will suit you the most, go for the colors that will make you feel good about your feelings.

Fashion that makes you feel good about yourself is the right fashion as the right fashion always allows the person to show its most authentic side of his or her personality.

This real fashion still exists in the 20th century and is being practiced by the artists and performers to present their ideas in front of you.

The fashion that asks you to manipulate your thoughts and ask you to change are those toxic advertisements which are just convincing you to shape according to their products and buy it so that they can have the huge profit margin.

4. Choose the character you want to play

There are always some clothes in our wardrobe that we don't wear that often. It is like when we are buying them we think we might wear them but at the end we end up not wearing them that often.

We have this habit of wearing certain clothes so often and forget about having variety. This happens very unknowingly. This used to happen with me a lot, I had certain clothes that I wore the least and got a huge portion of my budget consumed in buying that clothes.

The second thing that I noticed was that I usually used to think that I will wear this dress or I should start wearing this style but used to end up wearing that particular style or dress once or twice. Last to last year I thought I should wear long loose dresses in summer, this will be a change in my style also and I will be having the variety in my presentation. So I got a beautiful dress from the market but unfortunately I ended up not wearing it for that whole one year. After that, I actually forgot that I even have this dress. This kind of incident happened many times with me until I figured out this way of thinking pattern in choosing the clothes to wear from my wardrobe and now I will be sharing that technique with you all which allowed me to pick all type of the clothes from my wardrobe or buy them and also wear them all more often.

Now one thing that would come to your mind being a fashionista is that you would not look that fashionable if you would wear certain clothes so often. Wearing all sorts of clothes makes you look like having a lot of variety.

Styling is one of the most powerful tool in the fashion world as it allows you to wear certain clothes in so many different styles and in such a way that every time it gives you a completely different look with those same clothes. It is like a magic, a very creative process.

I call this technique as 'choosing your character' because it allows you to choose a character for the day which you would be playing. It is really fun and makes you analyze the whole day and choose the outfit to wear that day accordingly.

I was very unhappy from this one thing that used to happen with me, it was those clothes in my wardrobe that costed me some good price and I used to not be abled to wear them because I thought that I didn't get a suitable occasion to wear them. Then I figured out the solution as to think in the form of characters. So I started picking a character that I would be in for the day and then it became really easy for me to choose the outfit for the day in a more creative way.

Picking a character do not means that we would feel like wearing the same type of clothes, it is like that that sometimes we want to look very feminine and classy like Marilyn Monroe, sometimes we want to look bold and strong lady like the characters in sex in the city and sometimes wants to in nice casuals like Justine Bieber style, I love to say this way.

Let's understand it through some situations.
So I divide my analysis under three types:-
  i.   *Possible situations*
  ii.   *Solutions for situation*
  iii. *Situation ready*

1. If a situation is such where you and all your girlfriends decide to go out and have fun all day. Lets take it, your girlfriends decide to visit some amusement park. Now in this situation, you need to analyze the whole day, need to analyze the requirements your outfit would need to have so that you look fashionable, good and be comfortable at the same time.

Analise the situations by considering the place you gonna be
        (i) Possible situation

a. A lot of walking
b. Really shiny sun

Thinking about what you can have to be at your best
 (ii) *Solution for situation*
   a. Shoes for comfortable walking
   b. Can have comfortable lower
   c. Need scarf for protection

Finally, the third point gives you the idea of what you will prefer to wear in such a situation.

 (iii) *Situation ready*
   a. Have a **stylish top** to look fashionable
   b. Can have **a long jacket** for add fun in the look
   c. Will have **cargo** as lower for being comfortable
   d. And have **white sneakers**
   e. Keep a **hat** for protection

By dividing the information in this way we get an idea of the the most basic things we would prefer personally in this kind of situation. You get to know your preferences and the basic needs for your outfit by dividing your preferences in such a manner and your outfit is ready for the most possible situations and you could be completely comfortable and fashionable all at the same time.
You will have a rough idea of things you would need to add in your wardrobe for being situation ready for any such type of outing.
The third point in the list gives you the most basic items you need to have in your wardrobe. These items are the items that will pop up

the very first time in your mind when you have to get ready for such type of outing as these are your personalized items that you will prefer. This prevents you from having anything unnecessary in your closet which you won't be wearing and will help you save your money by not letting you spend on unnecessary clothes.

More similar situation like above can be like going out on the picnic, trecking, visiting any monumental place and many more.

For any similar situations, you are completely ready with the most basic outfit. To add some fun to your look you can search Pinterest or Instagram for some creative ideas, you will get some ideas for adding some fun elements to your outfit.

Let's get some more situations

2. If you have a plan to go out to meet the guy you like and it is a sort date where you would probably have a good conversation but it is not that typical fancy date with a lot of expenses. Now in this situation, you don't want to look overdone and neither underdone but want to look captivating.
Let's analyze the situation

> (i) Possible situation
>> a. Get for brunch
>> b. Can have a walk
>> c. A romantic situation might occur...<3

> (ii) solution for situation
>> a. Look romantic
>> b. Not to overdo but to look cute

c. for a walk and to look comfortable need to have flats as footwear

(iii)Situation ready
a. can have flowers **long dress**
b. have **bellies** as footwear

now you can add any beautiful printed long dress and bellies in your wardrobe to get yourself ready to present yourself for any romantic meeting. To add some fun elements, can add some jewelry like a small pendant or simple earrings or can get a beautiful hairstyle.

3. office look is so much important to consider. If there is any meeting and you need to be in complete formals. Sometimes it just became so important to wear formals and sometimes we feel like having formals at our workplace. Having formals are one of the most amazing ways to show your personality in terms of your strength and your attitude towards your work in handling it. Coco Chanel was an amazing lady to bring revolution in fashion style of ladies in the area of formal wear, she made clothes comfortable and so beautiful for ladies and became so popular among high class working ladies.

Let's analyze the situation

(j) Possible situation
a. Long hours of sitting/work
b. Can have meetings
c. Have presentation
d. Site visit

(ii) solution for situation
   a. Look attentive
   b. presentable
   c. average height heels
   d. comfortable outfit if a site visit

(iii)Situation ready
   a. can have **formals**, respective to your workplace
   b. have **black heels** as footwear

In the above situation I have not mentioned " formals" in detail because the term formal wear varies according to the profession, but still the basic formals includes plane shirt, pants or trousers, and blazers or coat .The type of formal you want to carry completely depends upon profession ,so it completely depends on your professional look requirements to what to include in your formal wear. That is why I haven't elaborated formal wear's elements. You can make your own list of formal wears according to your profession by diving the requirements under the above listing format and analyzing it according to your work and get your final formal clothes to list ready.

So now you have the complete picture of the outfits that you will need and with the help of the techniques you have the exact colors in your mind that you want in your wardrobe.

The next step is very very important for your budget wardrobe. This step is my most favorite step, that is shopping.
The most lovely step for all fashion lover!!!

So get yourself at the market and online stores and grab the best deals, bargain and get those clothes that you love.
And get them so that you can get them in your wardrobe.

WHAT to EXACTLY get into the wardrobe Finally!!!

Here I will give you the ready list of items needed to be in your budget wardrobe so that in this section you can be on an autopilot mode.

I am listing the minimum and the most basic items in this list that will fulfill all your basic need and will meet your fashion standards at the same time.

The choice of colors, patterns, and design can be completely made by using the techniques I explained earlier, so you will get the list of the items that you should not forget to add in your wardrobe.

After all this, you get the list of minimum items for wardrobe which will make you ready for most of the situations.

Slowly and gradually you can add extra items to your wardrobe and it will extend having a good number of items.

The listing begins as following

Lowers that you should include in your budget fashion wardrobe

- ✓ **2 jeans**
    - One dark colored
    - One light colored

- ✓ **2 formal pants**
    - Plane solid colored
    - Patterned or some design like check style or any style you like
- ✓ **3 comfortable lowers**
    - cargos
    - Pajamas
    - Shorts

Basic Tops and *tee* you should include in your budget fashion budget

- ✓ **2 shirts (formal)**
    - Plan
    - Printed

- ✓ **4 to 6 tops**
    - Try to get in the variety of colors

- ✓ **1 white t-shirt** must !!! (good fitting one)

✓ *2 t-shirt*
  - Polos
  - Casual

✓ *2 jackets*
  - 1 leather jacket
  - Denim jacket
  - Or can have an embroidery jacket

✓ *4 to 5 sweaters*

✓ *1 overcoat*

✓ *2 mufflers*

✓ *4 dresses*

  - 1 long dress
  - 1 midi type dress
  - 1 or 2 sexy party dress

✓ *3 scarfs*

Footwears that your budget fashion wardrobe should have

✓ **Boots**
  - Prefer knee length

- ✓ **Good walking shoes**

- ✓ **Flat sandals**
  - Simple classic style

- ✓ **Heels**
  - Wedges
  - Pencil heels (minimum 4 inches)
  - Can be black in color

EXTRAS basic items that you should include in your budget fashion wardrobe

- ✓ **1 classic bag**
  - Size should be according to your average requirement space.

- ✓ **Jumpsuits**

- ✓ **Designer lowers**

- ✓ **Beautiful bralets(really important !!)**

- ✓ **1 or 2 cultural dresses**

- ✓ **Jackets**

- ✓ **Special dresses**

- ✓ **Lots of junk jewelry**

The final strategy to keep in mind when you think of shopping next time

- Get the character in your mind, so that you have the character for which accordingly you will prepare your outfit.
- Set the color in your mind according to the moods. I will suggest you to choose colors which will make you feel cheerful and full of energy.

- Check the requirements. It is important to check your wardrobe so to have the knowledge of which basic items from the list is not in your wardrobe yet.

- When done with all this, it is time to add fun elements, that is to add 'extras' to your wardrobe. And don't forget to Choose the extras according to your characters.

- Final step and the last step, go out for the shopping because every detail is in your head now and you all you have to do is hunt for those stuff, arrange them in your budget and get them in your wardrobe finally to make it fashionable.

These all ways and technique will help you prevent yourself from buying the clothes that you think you will wear but never end up wearing them because those requirements are already fulfilled by your wardrobe, in this way most of the time we spend the huge part of our budget on things which don't fit in our unique fashion preferences. This will help you to spend your budget in your own type of fashion and highlight your beauty and prevent you from spending money on marketing fashion which is being done just for their own profits. Finally no more manipulative market victims and being the real fashion hunters of your own unique stylish personality.

www.ingramcontent.com/pod-product-compliance
Lightning Source LLC
Chambersburg PA
CBHW031334250726

48656CB00005B/2115